Britannica LEARNING LIBRARY

Creatures of the Waters

Encounter fascinating animals that live in and around water

ENCYCLOPÆDIA

Britannica®

CHICAGO   LONDON   NEW DELHI   PARIS   SEOUL   SYDNEY   TAIPEI   TOKYO

Creatures of the Waters

I N T R O D U C T I O N

How did the 'dabbling duck' get its name? What fish can leap up waterfalls? Is a sponge a plant or an animal? What animals can live both in water and on land?

In *Creatures of the Waters,* you'll discover answers to these questions and many more. Through pictures, articles, and fun facts, you'll learn about the great diversity of animal life found in waters around the world.

To help you on your journey, we've provided the following signposts in *Creatures of the Waters*:

■ **Subject Tabs**—The coloured box in the upper corner of each right-hand page will quickly tell you the article subject.

■ **Search Lights**—Try these mini-quizzes before and after you read the article and see how much - *and how quickly* - you can learn. You can even make this a game with a reading partner. (Answers are upside down at the bottom of one of the pages.)

■ **Did You Know?**—Check out these fun facts about the article subject. With these surprising 'factoids', you can entertain your friends, impress your teachers, and amaze your parents.

■ **Picture Captions**—Read the captions that go with the photos. They provide useful information about the article subject.

■ **Vocabulary**—New or difficult words are in **bold type**. You'll find them explained in the Glossary at the end of the book.

■ **Learn More!**—Follow these pointers to related articles in the book. These articles are listed in the Table of Contents and appear on the Subject Tabs.

Britannica LEARNING LIBRARY

Have a great trip!

Creatures of the Waters

TABLE OF CONTENTS

Which of the following can be said about an albatross?
a) It spends most of its time on land.
b) It eats other birds.
c) It goes to land only to lay eggs.

Albatrosses use their long wings to soar and glide on air currents. They can stay in the air for hours without flapping their wings. The black-browed albatross, shown here in flight, has a dark marking around the eye that makes it look as though it is frowning.

Forever Gliding

The albatross is an amazing seabird. It spends most of its life soaring above the water. The only time albatrosses ever go ashore is when they lay eggs and raise their chicks. Groups (called 'colonies') of the birds build nests on isolated Antarctic islands. A single large white egg is laid in a bowl-shaped nest built from plants and soil. Sometimes the nest is just a patch of bare ground.

Scientists measuring an albatross' wingspread.
© Wolfgang Kaehler/Corbis

A young albatross grows slowly. It takes at least four months for it to develop all the feathers it will need to fly. Once it's able to fly, the albatross will spend the next five to ten years out at sea. The albatross can glide for days at a time, without flapping its long narrow wings. To stay in the air like this, it needs windy weather. In calm weather the albatross has trouble keeping its heavy body in the air, so it rests on the water and floats like a cork. It feeds on small **squid** and fish. But it will also follow fishing boats and eat scraps that are thrown overboard.

Some kinds of albatrosses are brown, but most of them are white with some brown or black markings on their bodies or wings. Albatrosses are the largest of all flying birds. In fact, the wandering albatross has the largest wingspread amongst living birds. The wings of a wandering albatross can measure 3.4 metres from tip to tip.

Albatrosses live very long lives and are one of the few species of bird that die of old age.

LEARN MORE! READ THESE ARTICLES…
DUCKS • GULLS • PENGUINS

DID YOU KNOW?

In the past, sailors believed albatrosses had special powers. They believed that killing the bird would bring bad luck.

Answer: c) It goes to land only to lay eggs.

A male wood duck is easily identifiable by his purple and green head, his reddish-brown breast flecked with white, and his bronze sides.
© Gary W. Carter/Corbis

SEARCH LIGHT

Unscramble these words that have to do with a duck.
wsmimre
nblbiadg
dlwaed

8

Dabblers, Divers, and Perchers

Ducks are champion swimmers and are at home almost anywhere near water. Some feed and nest in streams and ponds. Others live near deep wide lakes. Some make their homes on rocky cliffs by the ocean.

There are three kinds of duck:

'**Dabbling** ducks' put their heads under water to eat plants that grow there. This way of feeding is called 'dabbling'. They build their nests in hollows near the water. There they also eat plants and insects found near the shore. Dabbling ducks can fly very fast.

'Diving ducks' dive deep down into the water to find things to eat. They mostly eat fish. They are very strong swimmers.

'Perching ducks' make nests in trees and hold on to the branches with their long-clawed toes. This is called perching. Some may perch on the tall stalks that grow over marshy ponds.

All ducks are graceful fliers and swimmers. But on the ground they waddle from side to side, moving slowly in a funny, jerky way. You usually don't see a duck waddling too far away from water.

In winter many ducks fly south, where the water is warmer and there's more to eat. But icy cold water doesn't bother them. A thick inner layer of soft fluffy feathers called 'down' keeps them warm. And their bigger outer feathers help too. They're **waterproof**. Feathers are a duck's raincoat. Every year ducks lose their old feathers, and new feathers grow in. This is called 'moulting'. Until the new feathers grow, ducks can't fly. So they hide in the grass or on the water to keep safe from enemies.

© Roger Wilmshurst—Frank Lane Picture Agency/Corbis

© Royalty-Free/Corbis

(Top) A dabbling gadwall duck; (bottom) young girl holding a fluffy duckling.

LEARN MORE! READ THESE ARTICLES…
GEESE • GULLS • SWANS

Answer: wswimmre = swimmer
nbiblads = dabbling
dlwaed = waddle

Fine-Feathered Travellers

Geese are found virtually everywhere. There's the wild Canada goose, and halfway around the world is the snow goose of Siberia. There is the **pied** goose, which lives 'down under' in Australia. The rarely seen Hawaiian goose lives out in the middle of the Pacific Ocean. The little brant goose nests in very cold Arctic areas. The wild goose called the greylag is found in Europe.

Geese spend a lot of time in the water. Like ducks, they have a coat of oil on their feathers that keeps them from getting too wet. And the soft feathers beneath, called 'down', keep them warm even in the iciest of waters. Down is so good at keeping things warm that people often use it in ski jackets and in duvets. It's also good in pillows because it's so soft.

Geese are fairly large birds, often standing a metre tall despite their short legs. Geese may look somewhat silly when they waddle on land. But their **sturdy** legs actually help them walk more steadily than ducks or swans do.

Geese have webbed feet that make them strong swimmers. They are also powerful fliers. They can make especially long flights during their annual **migrations** to their winter feeding grounds. You may see groups of geese travelling south in the autumn in lines that make a V shape. This formation helps keep them from getting tired as they fly because each goose gets a lift from the air flowing off the goose ahead.

(Top) Mother goose nuzzling her gosling (young goose); (bottom) snow geese flying in a V formation.

LEARN MORE! READ THESE ARTICLES…
DUCKS • GULLS • SWANS

DID YOU KNOW?
Some people keep geese as guards. Geese make loud honking cries when danger appears. After chasing the enemy away, they cackle triumphantly.

10

SEARCH LIGHT

How
do people
use
down feathers?

A Canada goose flies close to the water.

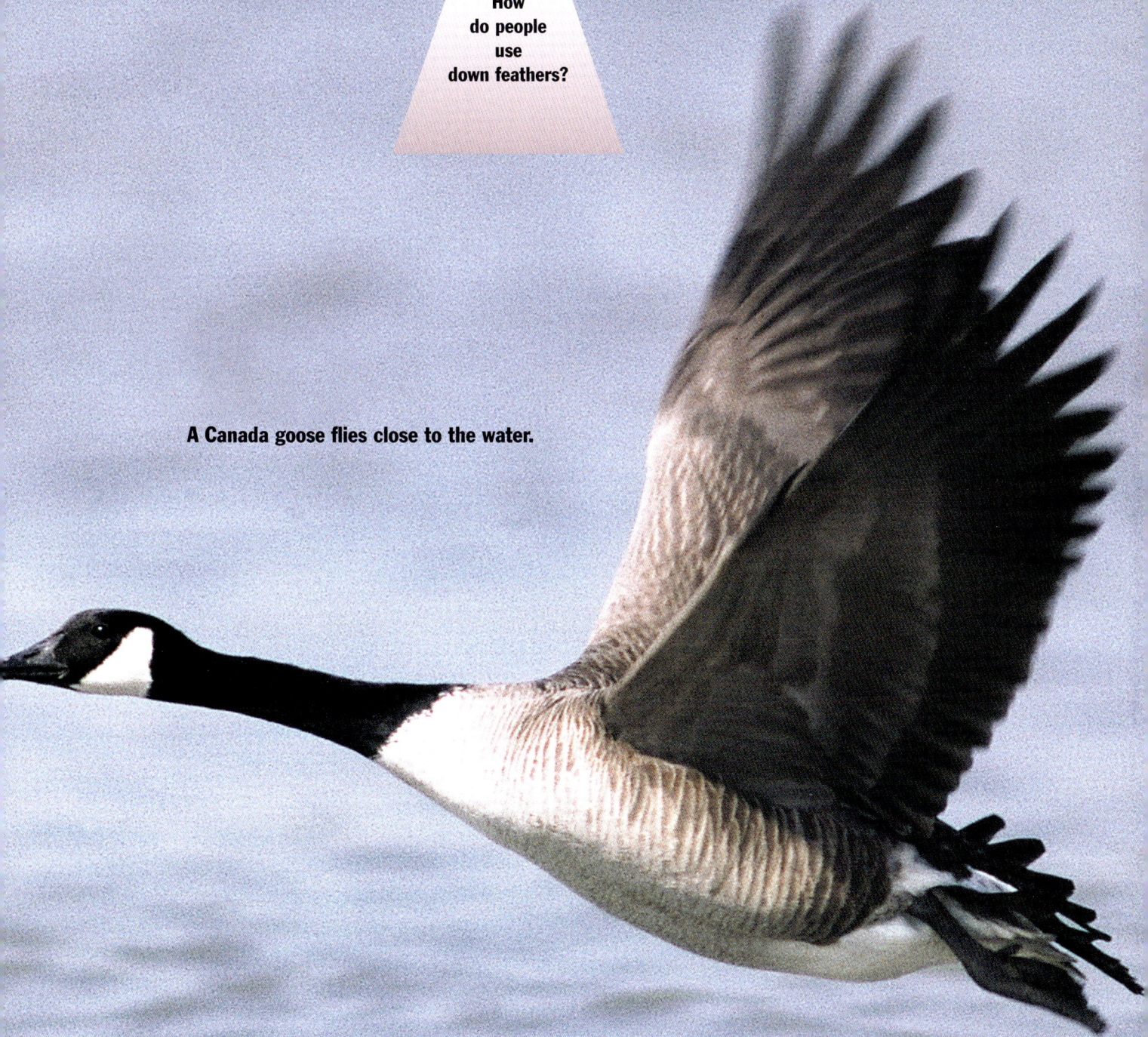

Answer: People use down to stuff pillows, duvets, and ski jackets because the feathers are soft and very warm.

Gulls are among the most common water birds of ocean and coastal zones worldwide. Some gulls travel enormous distances between their summer and winter homes.

SEARCH LIGHT

How are gulls helpful to humans?

The Ocean's Clean-up Crew

A fishing boat chugs back into the harbour with its day's catch. The gulls follow close behind. They know that the fishermen will be throwing treats overboard as they empty the bait bag and clean the deck. The gulls dip into the waves to scoop up bits of food. They fill the air with their excited cries. This often happens when they are fighting over something good to eat.

Along the shore, gulls are helpful to the people who clean beaches and harbours. They swoop down to pick up messy things. Gulls eat almost anything, from dead fish to crisps and scraps of hot dogs. And they clear away lots of insects too.

Gulls eat all day long. They have to just to stay alive. Gulls are big birds that fly great distances. While flying, they use up a lot of energy. Gulls can fly many kilometres without stopping. They can fly from one end of a country to the other. But all the time they're up there, they're looking down to see if they can find something to eat.

Gulls are good swimmers too. Their feet are webbed. The little stretches of skin between their toes make their feet act as paddles.

Gulls are also floaters. They stay on top of the water like a piece of wood does. On long trips over the ocean, they drop down onto the water and float while taking a nap.

Seagull stands on a rock.
© Guy Motil/Corbis

DID YOU KNOW?
The type of gull called Bonaparte's gull was named after Charles-Lucien Bonaparte, a nephew of the famous French emperor Napoleon Bonaparte. The younger Bonaparte spent much of his life studying the world's birds.

LEARN MORE! READ THESE ARTICLES…
ALBATROSSES • DUCKS • FISH

Answer: Gulls clean up a lot of food waste from beaches, harbours, picnic areas, tips, and car parks that would otherwise be left behind as rubbish.

Penguins are excellent divers and swimmers. Here, gentoo penguins enjoy a romp through the water.

SEARCH LIGHT

Do penguins have feathers?

Well-Dressed Swimmers

When a penguin swims, its light-coloured belly and dark-coloured back help hide it from enemies. From underneath, its light belly looks like the sky. This makes it hard for its enemy the leopard seal to see it. From above, its dark back looks like the dark water, which helps hide it from big hunting birds.

Penguins cannot fly, but they swim extremely well. The shape of their bodies, sort of like a submarine, lets them swim very fast. They use their short flat wings like flippers and practically fly through the water. In fact, they often leap out of the water and look as if they are trying to flap through the air.

There are 17 types of penguins. They live in Antarctica and along the cool portions of the coasts of Africa, New Zealand, Australia, and South America. Penguins have a thick layer of fat that helps to protect them from the cold. And although they don't look like they do, they actually have feathers all over their bodies. These short feathers also help to keep them warm.

Penguins' short legs give them an odd walk. They do, however, run quickly. Sometimes they'll build up speed and then slide on their bellies to travel quickly over ice and snow.

Penguins live in nesting **colonies**. These colonies can be enormous. Penguins return to the same place, the same nest, and the same partner every year - sometimes travelling long distances. Penguins use the Sun to help them find their direction. Most penguins build a nest on the ground with pebbles, mud, and vegetation. The females lay one or two eggs, and then both parents take turns looking after them.

Members of the emperor penguin species, the largest of the penguins.
© Tim Davis/Corbis

LEARN MORE! READ THESE ARTICLES...
ALBATROSSES • GULLS • SWANS

DID YOU KNOW?

Penguins are the only birds that can swim but not fly.

Answer: Like all birds, penguins have feathers. But theirs are so short and close to their bodies that the feathers look more like skin.

Birds of Beauty, Grace, and Speed

Ducks, geese, and swans are the three main kinds of waterfowl. Swans are the largest of the three, and they are also the fastest flyers and swimmers. They have a stately and dignified appearance when swimming on a pond.

Like the other waterfowl, swans have oily feathers that stay dry in the water. Their webbed feet make them strong swimmers. Swans are heavy-bodied birds that feed by dabbling - dipping the long neck into shallow water for plants. They don't dive for food. They have powerful wings for flying long distances.

Mother swan and cygnets.
© AFP/Corbis

The whistling swan and the trumpeter swan are found in North America, while the mute swan lives in Europe and Asia. These birds are white. South America is the home of the black-necked swan, while the beautiful black swan lives in Australia. It is the state emblem of Western Australia.

Swans make a variety of sounds. Even the mute swan often hisses or makes soft snoring sounds. It may even grunt sharply.

The male swan is called a 'cob'. The female is called a 'pen'. They look alike. A pair of swans usually stays together for life. The female swan lays about six pale eggs on a heap of plant material, while the male keeps close guard. The young swans are called 'cygnets'. They can run and swim just a few hours after they hatch. But father and mother swan look after them carefully for several months. Sometimes the cygnets will ride on their mother's back when they get tired from swimming or need protection from enemies.

LEARN MORE! READ THESE ARTICLES...
DUCKS • GEESE • GULLS

DID YOU KNOW?
E.B. White's *The Trumpet of the Swan* is a story about a voiceless swan that learns to play a trumpet.

SEARCH LIGHT

What's one way that ducks and swans are alike? How are they different?

A family of mute swans, with cygnets riding on their mother's back, swim along the water.
© Philip Perry—Frank Lane Picture Agency/Corbis

Answer: Both ducks and swans are water birds with oily feathers and webbed feet for swimming. But swans are considerably bigger than ducks. They fly and swim faster than ducks too.

SEARCH LIGHT

What's so special about amphibians? (Hint: Remember those Greek words.)

The Land-and-Water Dwellers

Millions of years ago, a group of fish began to breathe both in and out of the water. Eventually these fish made their way onto land and began to develop legs. These animals became amphibians, the ancestors of frogs, toads, and salamanders.

The word 'amphibian' comes from the Greek words *amphi*, which means 'both', and *bios*, which means 'life'. As their name suggests, amphibians live both in freshwater and on land.

Amphibians are cold-blooded animals. This means that an amphibian's body temperature generally matches the temperature around it. To warm up, amphibians often **bask** in the sun, and to cool off, they move into the shade. Amphibians must also stay near water. If their skin dries out, they will die.

There are three main groups of amphibian. The largest group includes the true frogs, tree frogs, and toads. True frogs have long hind legs and can swim and leap very well. Tree frogs have suction pads on their fingers and toes and can hold on to smooth surfaces. Toads have shorter legs than frogs, and their skin has a warty appearance.

The second group of amphibians is the salamanders, which have tails. The giant salamander of Japan and China is the largest of all amphibians. It can grow to a length of more than 1.5 metres.

The third group is the caecilians. These odd amphibians are rarely seen. They have long slender bodies with no arms or legs. They are also blind. A long flexible structure called a 'tentacle' sticks out next to each of their useless eyes. They use these tentacles to feel and sniff their way around.

LEARN MORE! READ THESE ARTICLES…
FISH • FROGS • TURTLES

Answer: Amphibians are one of the few groups of animals that can live comfortably both in the water and on the land.

Amazing Changing Amphibians

Frogs are amphibians. This means they can live both in water and on land. And they have a life cycle that takes place in both environments.

A mother frog lays her eggs in the water. In a few days tiny tadpoles, or polliwogs, wriggle out of the eggs. The tadpoles don't look like frogs at all. They have long tails for swimming and slits called **gills** for breathing.

As a tadpole grows into a frog, it changes in many ways. Its tail gets shorter and shorter until it disappears. At the same time, the frog grows front and hind legs. The hind feet have long toes with webs between them to help in swimming and leaping. Plus, the gills disappear and **lungs** develop. Once these changes are complete, the creature is ready to live on land as well as in the water. It's now a frog. For some kinds of frogs, this process of change takes just two months. For others, it may take as long as three years.

Red-eyed leaf frog tadpoles.
© Michael & Patricia Fogden/Corbis

A frog has smooth moist skin. Its eyes are so big that they seem about to pop out of its head. These eyes help it find food. Its hind legs are more than twice as long as its front ones. The frog travels in great leaps on these long strong legs.

Frogs are closely related to toads. What's the difference between a frog and a toad? Well, a toad's skin is dry and bumpy. Its legs are short, so it can only hop, not leap. And toads spend more of their time on land than frogs do.

LEARN MORE! READ THESE ARTICLES…
AMPHIBIANS • FISH • TURTLES

SEARCH LIGHT

Unscramble the following words that relate to frogs.
daploet
sligl
traew

The tree frog has long legs and sticky sucker-like disks on its feet for climbing.
© Darren Maybury—Eye Ubiquitous/Corbis

Answer: daploet = tadpole
sligl = gills
traew = water

Today, many alligators and crocodiles are in danger of becoming extinct. One reason is
that many are killed each year for sport or for their skins, which are used to make purses,
shoes, and belts. These crocodiles are lying in the grass near Moramanga, Madagascar.
© Wolfgang Kaehler/Corbis

22

Modern Dinosaurs

If you're looking for reptiles that have been around since the days of the dinosaurs, try alligators and crocodiles. These large lizard-like animals are related to the giant reptiles of the past.

Alligators and crocodiles are closely related. They look a lot alike, but alligators have a broad flat head with a rounded **snout**. Most crocodiles have a narrow, pointed snout. When a crocodile closes its mouth, the fourth tooth on each side of its lower jaw sticks out. Crocodiles are larger than alligators. They range from 2 to more than 6 metres long, while most alligators are about 1.8 to 2.4 metres long.

Alligators in the Okefenokee Swamp, Georgia, U.S.
© David Muench/Corbis

Alligators and most crocodiles live along the edges of large bodies of freshwater such as lakes, swamps, and rivers. They spend a lot of time in the water, but they can also be found on land near the water. Large adults can stay under water for over an hour without breathing.

Both animals have long snouts, powerful tails, and thick skin with bony plates underneath. Their eyes, ears, and nostrils are located on top of their long heads. Alligators and crocodiles often float with only their eyes and noses showing.

Crocodiles can be found in **tropical** swamps and rivers in Asia, Australia, Africa, and South America. Alligators are less widespread. The American alligator lives in the south-eastern United States. In South America there are various alligators called caimans. The Chinese alligator lives in the Yangtze River and is smaller than the American alligator.

Adult alligators and crocodiles eat mostly fish, small mammals, and birds. Sometimes they may kill deer or cattle. Crocodiles are more likely than alligators to attack humans, though alligators will attack if cornered.

DID YOU KNOW?

There are saltwater crocodiles living in northern Australia and Southeast Asia. Australians call their crocodiles 'salties'.

LEARN MORE! READ THESE ARTICLES…
AMPHIBIANS • MANATEES • TURTLES

Answer: FALSE. Though they are related, alligators and crocodiles are two different animals.

Find and correct the error in the following sentence: Anacondas kill their prey with a poisonous bite.

A Tight Squeeze

The giant anaconda is one of the longest and heaviest snakes in the world. But this South American animal is not poisonous. The anaconda kills its prey by squeezing it so hard that it cannot breathe.

The anaconda spends most of its time in water. When an animal goes to a river to drink, the anaconda grabs it. If the prey is large, the snake wraps itself around the animal and can choke it. The anaconda then drags the body into the water to keep it away from jaguars and biting ants that would be attracted to the **carcass**. When an anaconda eats a large animal, it gets so stuffed that it lies still for weeks to digest its meal!

Giant anaconda.
© Z. Leszczynski/Animals Animals

There are two types of anaconda. The yellow anaconda is the smaller of the two. It is tan or greenish yellow with large black markings across its back and black blotches along its sides. Yellow anacondas are found in the southern Amazon River area. The giant anaconda is twice as big as the yellow anaconda. It's olive green with black spots. The giant anaconda lives in the South American tropics east of the Andes Mountains and on the Caribbean island of Trinidad. Giant anacondas can measure over 10 metres long.

Despite its size, a giant anaconda is not really violent. Scientists can simply pick up an anaconda and carry it off. But it may take several of them to lift the snake, especially if it just ate!

LEARN MORE! READ THESE ARTICLES…
ALLIGATORS AND CROCODILES • AMPHIBIANS • SHARKS

A yellow anaconda lies on a log at the edge of the water. Although the anaconda spends much of its time in water, it may also crawl on land and even climb into trees to catch birds.
© Joe McDonald/Corbis

DID YOU KNOW?
Like most snakes, anacondas swallow their food whole. They can open their mouths wide enough to fit around an entire goat.

Answer: Anacondas kill their prey by squeezing it.

Taking Their Time

Turtles are known as slow-moving animals. They were around during the age of dinosaurs more than 100 million years ago. Dinosaurs are gone now, but turtles are still here. Slow but steady wins the race!

Like the dinosaurs, turtles are reptiles. There are nearly 250 kinds of turtle in the world today. All turtles breathe air at least part of the time,

Three painted turtles perched on a rock.
© William Manning/Corbis

even sea turtles, which spend almost their whole life in the ocean. In addition to the ocean, turtles can live in ponds, lakes, or rivers. Other turtles live in forests or even hot desert sands, far away from water. Some people refer to land turtles as 'tortoises'.

Turtles come in all sizes. Some are no more than 10 centimetres long. At the other end of the scale, the Atlantic leatherback turtle may weigh as much as 680 kilos.

Even sea turtles go ashore to lay their eggs. The newly hatched baby turtles are completely on their own. They scramble from their nest under the sand and walk on their tiny new flippers to the water.

Land and sea turtles can take care of themselves because they carry their houses with them wherever they go. Their houses are their shells. Some turtles can close their shells completely. The snapping turtle can't, but it has a powerful bite for protection.

No matter where they live, turtles don't need to hunt for food or water all the time. Some have a special place inside their bodies where they can store water. And they can store food in the form of fat. Turtles can live for days or even weeks without having anything to eat or drink.

SEARCH LIGHT

Fill in the gap: Land turtles are sometimes called _____.

LEARN MORE! READ THESE ARTICLES...
AMPHIBIANS · FROGS · MOLLUSCS

A boy kneels to investigate a small turtle. Turtles are found in lakes, ponds, salt marshes, rivers, forests, and even deserts.
© Ariel Skelley/Corbis

Answer: Land turtles are sometimes called tortoises.

Citizens of the Waters

A fish is a cold-blooded animal that has a backbone, lives in water, and breathes by means of **gills**. It normally has two pairs of fins in place of arms and legs, as well as several other fins. Most fish are covered with **scales**.

Fish are fascinating in their variety. The sea horse looks something like a tiny horse standing on its tail. Flounders are as flat as a dinner plate. The rabbitfish, a small relative of the shark, has a head and teeth resembling those of a rabbit. Anglerfish carry their own 'fishing rod' to catch other fish. An extended part of the back fin has wormlike pieces of flesh at the tip, which are the 'bait'. Anglers of the deep sea have bait that lights up to attract victims.

Size differs as much as shape. Some Philippine gobies reach an adult size of less than one and a quarter centimetres. The whale shark, the largest of all fishes, reaches 50 metres in length and weighs about 18 tonnes.

Fish swim mainly by sideways movements of the body and tail. The fins are used for balancing, steering, and braking. To move quickly from a resting position, some fish shoot a stream of water out of the gills, which causes them to lunge forward. The fastest swimmers, such as the tuna, can travel 48 kilometres per hour.

Most fish continue to grow as long as they live. Fish that live to an old age can become very large. Carp are among this group. They may live 100 years!

LEARN MORE! READ THESE ARTICLES…
CARP • SALMON • SHARKS

DID YOU KNOW?

Fish called mudskippers can crawl across mud flats and wet fields in search of food. Lungfish can burrow into mud when their pools dry up. They lie there, for months if necessary, until rain refills the pools.

SEARCH LIGHT

Fill in
the gap.
Fish
breathe through
_____.

Answer: Fish breathe through gills.

The Fishy Survivor

The common carp is a fish that lives along the muddy bottoms of ponds, lakes, and rivers. It swallows plants, insects, and anything else it finds to eat. It was first found in Asia but was later taken into Europe and North America. Some people like to eat carp.

Sometimes carp can live 100 years and grow to weigh 35 kilos or more. But not all carp grow that old or that heavy. The fish that are caught usually are under 10 years old and do not weigh more than 4.5 kilos.

The carp has a blunt nose and a small thick-lipped mouth. From its upper lip dangle two pairs of feelers that are called 'barbels'.

There are three kinds of common carp. The scale carp has large scales all over its wide heavy body. Its back is olive green, its sides are gold-coloured, and its belly is bright yellow. The mirror carp has only three or four rows of huge scales along its sides. The leather carp is almost without scales, but it has a very thick skin.

In some ways the carp is a **nuisance**. In hunting for food, the carp muddies the water. This affects the life of many plants and animals. A carp sometimes pushes more valuable fish away from their food and also eats their eggs. The carp has a habit of pulling out plants from their roots. This keeps ducks away. It is very difficult to get rid of carp. The fish can thrive even in dirty water and can also survive in very warm and very cold water.

Goldfish swimming in a bowl.
© Doug Wilson/Corbis

SEARCH LIGHT

True or false? Carp live in the ocean.

LEARN MORE! READ THESE ARTICLES…
FISH • PIRANHAS • SALMON

Colourful carp swim in a pond outside a restaurant in Japan. In Asia and Europe carp are often raised in ponds because it is possible to grow many fish in a small amount of water.
© Wolfgang Kaehler/Corbis

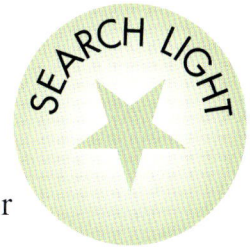

Answer: FALSE. They live in freshwater rivers, lakes, and ponds.

A Frightening Little Fish

The piranha is found in the rivers and lakes of South America. It is a meat-eating fish with long, triangular, razor-sharp teeth. When hungry, the piranha can be both bold and **savage**. But for such a frightening fish, it is not very big. Most are about the size of an adult's hand.

Some piranhas are silver in colour, with orange undersides. Others are almost totally black. All have blunt heads, saw-edged bellies, and strong jaws.

In the Amazon River, there are 20 different kinds of piranhas. The most famous is the red-bellied piranha. It has the strongest jaws and the sharpest teeth.

Why do you suppose that when water levels get low, piranhas hunt in larger schools than they would otherwise? (Hint: How much of your body can you fit underwater in the tub once you start letting the water out?)

When water levels are low, this piranha hunts in schools of more than 100 fish. Many schools join in the feast if a large animal has been attacked. But normally red-bellied piranhas prefer **prey** only slightly larger than themselves.

Red-bellied piranha.
© Kevin Schafer/Corbis

Usually a group of red-bellied piranhas swim around together in search of prey. The moment the prey is found, the fish signal each other. Piranhas have excellent hearing, so it's possible that they signal each other with sounds. Each fish in the group has a chance to take a bite and then swim away, making way for the others.

Most piranhas never kill large animals, and they almost never kill humans. The smell of blood attracts piranhas, but most of them feed on what is left by others rather than making fresh kills. For this reason their reputation for being ferocious is not deserved.

LEARN MORE! READ THESE ARTICLES…
CARP • FISH • SHARKS

Groups of piranhas hide out and chase and attack fish that swim by.
© John Madere/Corbis

DID YOU KNOW?
The name 'piranha' comes from the Portuguese words for 'fish' and 'tooth'.

Answer: When river water levels are low, there's less room for fish to spread out, so piranhas have to hunt together in large groups.

DID YOU KNOW?

Each generation of salmon returns to the same river, to the same spot, to lay their eggs every year. So a salmon's parents, grandparents, and great grandparents all chose the same river.

Leaping Up the Waterfall

True or false? Salmon travel upstream against the river current to lay their eggs.

These fish aren't going down a waterfall. They're going up! Not much can stop these big strong salmon - not even a waterfall. The salmon are swimming up the river to return to the quiet waters where they hatched. They're returning in order to spawn - that is, to lay their own eggs. They started their journey far out in the sea.

Somehow the salmon manage to find the river they are looking for. Night and day they swim on. They eat nothing at all after getting into their river. Finally, they reach the waters where they came from.

Male sockeye salmon.
© Natalie Fobes/Corbis

We don't know how salmon can find their way on this long trip up the river. But we know what they do when they reach the end. At the top of the stream, the mother salmon digs a long hole with her tail and **snout**. She fills the hole with thousands of tiny eggs. She covers the eggs with sand to keep them safe.

The eggs hatch. When the baby salmon are about as long as your finger, they are big enough to start the swim to the ocean. They float backward down the long river - tails first and heads last! They seem to steer better that way.

Many of the babies never reach the ocean because there are too many enemies. Birds, bears, and bigger fish along the way love to eat them. The salmon that do reach the ocean will one day start the long hard trip up the river.

LEARN MORE! READ THESE ARTICLES…
CARP • FISH • SHARKS

These Pacific salmon are trying to leap up a waterfall of the Brooks River in Katmai National Park, Alaska, U.S., to spawn upstream.
© Galen Rowell/Corbis

Predators of the Sea

When the first dinosaurs walked on Earth, sharks were already swimming in the sea. The dinosaurs are long gone, but sharks are still a force to be reckoned with.

Great white sharks, in particular, are feared as man-eaters. It's hard to fight them, because they are so strong and fast in the water. Their tough skin is protected by tiny toothlike scales. In their big mouths are rows and rows of sharp teeth that rip like the edge of a saw. Sharks continue to grow teeth all their lives. A great white can make a quick meal out of almost anything!

The hammerhead shark can also be dangerous. Don't be fooled by its awkward-looking rectangle of a head. In general, most shark attacks take place in shallow water, where sharks sometimes go to hunt for fish. A hungry shark can easily mistake a human arm or leg for a tasty fish.

Most kinds of sharks are not dangerous to people. This includes the largest shark of all, the whale shark. Whale sharks can be 15 metres long, but they feed on small fish and on tiny life forms called plankton. Other sharks eat fish of all sizes. The shark appears out of nowhere, often from below, to take its prey by surprise.

Did you know that a shark has to keep swimming all the time? Its body is made in such a way that if it doesn't swim, it will sink to the bottom of the sea. Good thing sharks know how to sleep while they swim!

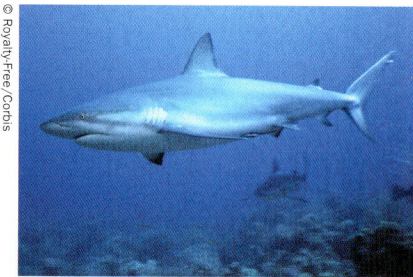

(Top) Scalloped hammerhead shark; (bottom) swimming shark.

© Amos Nachoum/Corbis

© Royalty-Free/Corbis

LEARN MORE! READ THESE ARTICLES...
DEEP-SEA LIFE • FISH • PIRANHAS

SEARCH LIGHT

Find and correct the error in the following sentence: Hammerhead sharks got their name because they bash their prey over the head.

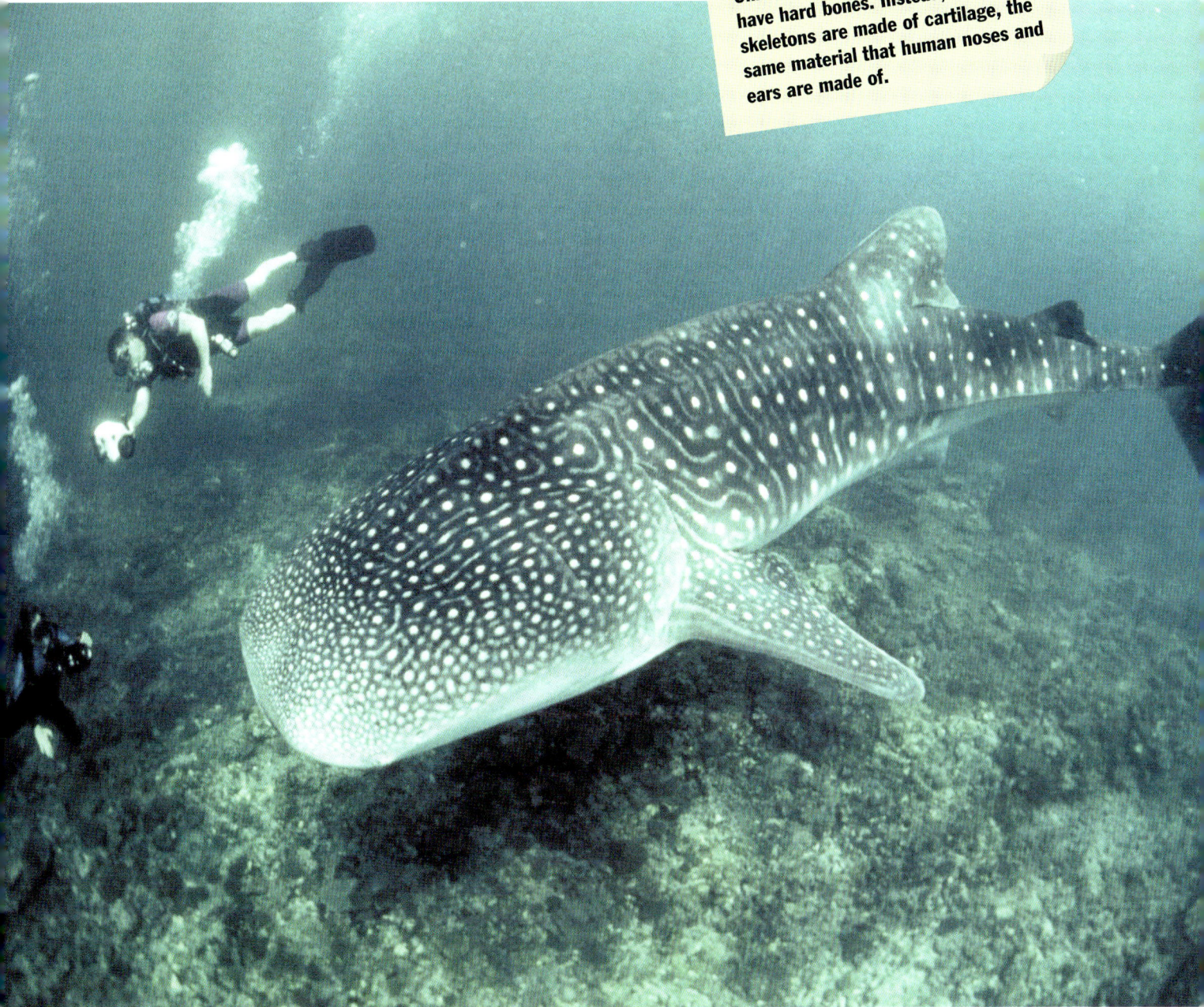

Scuba divers photograph a whale shark. Whale sharks usually swim slowly near the surface and have even been hit by ships.

© Jeffrey L. Rotman/Corbis

Answer: Hammerhead sharks got their name because their heads look like hammers.

There is an amazing variety of sea life on and around the Great Barrier Reef. There are about 400 types of hard coral, about 215 types of birds, and more than 1,500 types of fish, many with bright colours and unusual shapes.

© Australian Picture Library/Corbis

DID YOU KNOW?

The Great Barrier Reef is the largest structure ever built by living things. It is longer than the Great Wall of China and much wider.

Builders in the Sea

SEARCH LIGHT

★

Two parts of the animal are called coral. What are they?

A coral is a soft little sea animal that looks like a bit of jelly. It is no bigger than the end of your little finger. At one end it has a mouth surrounded by little arms called 'tentacles'. The tentacles gather food. When they touch a tiny plant or animal floating nearby, they pull these inside the mouth.

The baby coral swims through the water until it finds a place to build its house, and then it never swims again. Using special glue from inside its body, it sticks itself to a rock or to another piece of coral. Once it is stuck, it starts to build itself a house with a juice from its body that turns into a kind of stone. The hard little shell houses are called coral too.

© Royalty-Free/Corbis

© Royalty-Free/Corbis

(Top) Orange cup coral; (bottom) yellow and gray coral.

In the ocean where the water is warm, the coral grows in lovely ocean gardens. It grows in just about every colour and shape you can think of. It may grow to look like lace, a fan, a leaf, a brain, the horns of a deer, or a ribbon.

One day a bud will grow on the coral. This bud grows into a new coral animal. After many years there are so many coral houses built on top of one another and next to each other that they become a great wall called a 'reef'.

Sometimes coral may grow together to form a reef hundreds of kilometres long. The largest coral reef in the world is the Great Barrier Reef near Australia. It is more than 2,000 kilometres long.

LEARN MORE! READ THESE ARTICLES…
DEEP-SEA LIFE • MOLLUSCS • SPONGES

★ Answer: Coral refers to the soft jelly-like animal living inside the hard shell, as well as to the shell itself. People also call many of these shells stuck together 'coral'.

Flashing Lights!

SEARCH LIGHT

Fill in
the gap:
The deepest
part of the ocean
is called the
_____ zone.

It is very dark deep below the surface of the oceans of the world. This dark area is called the 'abyssal zone'. It is a black, soundless place where the water is very still. This zone lies thousands of metres below the water's surface.

You wouldn't think it, but there are many kinds of living things to be found in the abyss. For a very long time, people believed that nothing could live down there because there isn't any light. But scientists who investigated the deep sea found plenty of life!

Many forms of life were discovered near cracks on the ocean floor. These are called 'rift communities'. The huge cracks, or fissures, are between two of the **plates** that make up the Earth's crust. These fissures are hot-water vents that raise the temperature of the water around them. The fissures are rich in **minerals**.

Deep-sea anglerfish.
© Bruce Robinson/Corbis

Deep-sea animals include certain kinds of squid, octopuses, worms, and fish. Because it is difficult to study animals at such levels, not much is known about their behaviour or surroundings. But it is known that deep-sea animals have special features that allow them to live in conditions in which other animals could not. These features are called **adaptations**.

Many deep-sea fish and other creatures flash with their own lights. This ability to give off light is called 'bioluminescence'. It is an adaptation for living in the darkness of the deep sea. Some deep-sea animals have coloured lights on different parts of the body. Their bodies keep flashing on and off. It is possible that the animals are speaking to each other with their lights.

LEARN MORE! READ THESE ARTICLES...
MOLLUSCS • OCTOPUSES • SPONGES

Tube worms are just one example of the many types of life found deep in the ocean. Tube worms are large red worms that live inside white tubes that are attached to the ocean floor.
© F. Grassle, Woods Hole Oceanographic Institution

Answer: The deepest part of the ocean is called the abyssal zone.

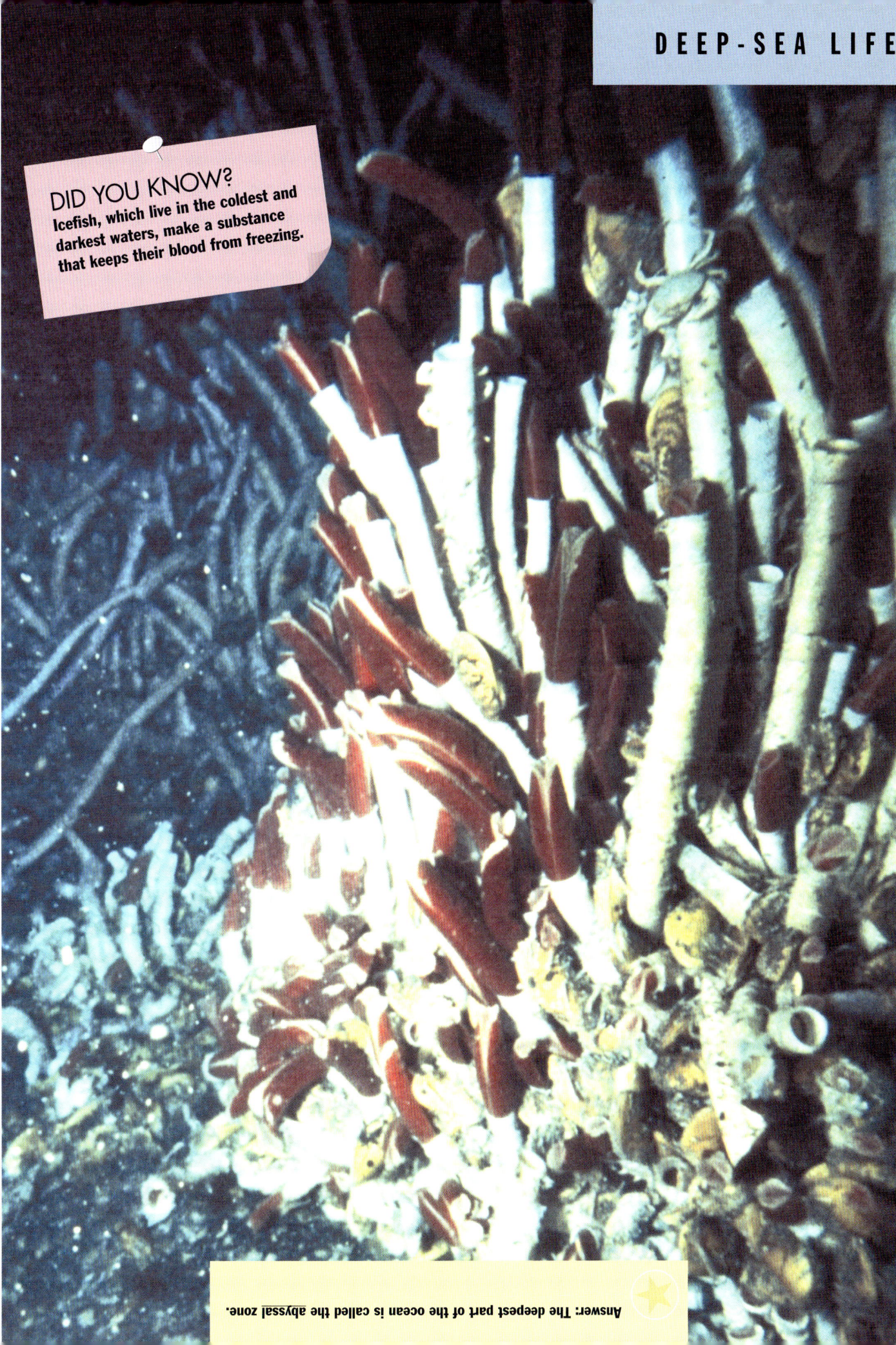

SEARCH LIGHT

Can you think of one way that jellyfish and fish are similar? What's one way that they're different?

Boneless Blobs of the Sea

A jellyfish is not a fish at all. Unlike fish it has no bones, and most of its body is like jelly. It does not have a brain or a heart. What it does have is a set of **tentacles** that can sting its prey - or a person!

Jellyfish are related to corals and sea anemones. They can be found in all oceans. There are about 200 kinds of jellyfish, in different forms, sizes, and colours. Some jellyfish are barely large enough to be seen. Others can be more than two metres around. Jellyfish may be transparent or brown, pink, white, or blue. Some kinds glow in the dark sea.

Jellyfish in dark waters.
© Jeffrey L. Rotman/Corbis

A jellyfish usually has the shape of an umbrella. It can have a few or many tentacles. Sometimes it has simple eyes around the edge of the 'umbrella'. The mouth and the stomach are in the middle of the 'umbrella'. The jellyfish has simple muscles on the underside that **contract** the body, much like the closing of an umbrella. This helps it swim.

Inside the tentacles of a jellyfish are poisonous stinging cells. These cells can stun small animals, which the jellyfish then pulls into its mouth. Some jellyfish feed on tiny animals and plants that their bodies catch as they drift through the water.

Some jellyfish can be very dangerous to humans. Even a small sting from the jellyfish called sea wasps can cause death within a few minutes. It's best just to look at jellyfish from a distance and not get too close.

LEARN MORE! READ THESE ARTICLES…
CORAL • DEEP-SEA LIFE • OCTOPUSES

DID YOU KNOW?
Sometimes a jelly-like blob breaks away from a jellyfish and grows into another adult jellyfish.

Jellyfish sometimes sting swimmers who accidentally brush up against them in the water. Even dead jellyfish that have washed up on the beach can be dangerous and should not be touched.
© Danny Lehman/Corbis

Answer: The most obvious thing that jellyfish and fish share is their ocean home. One big difference between them is that jellyfish have no bones but fish do.

Shell-Dwelling Animals

There are many different shelled animals. The smallest live in shells as tiny as the letter 'O'. The largest, such as the giant squids, weigh more than two tonnes! Some of these animals belong to a group called 'molluscs'. And you might be surprised to know that there are about 100,000 kinds of them!

SEARCH LIGHT

Which of the following are molluscs?
- crabs
- snails
- prawns
- oysters
- squids

Most molluscs - such as snails, clams, oysters, and mussels - have shells. But some, such as octopuses and squid, have little or none at all. And not all kinds of animals with shells are molluscs. Crabs and lobsters have shells, but they are not molluscs.

Snail on a child's hand.
© Lance Nelson/Corbis

Although most molluscs live in the water, some are found on land. Snails live in forests and gardens.

Newborn molluscs are squishy and helpless. They need protection from enemies that would eat them. They get this protection from the shell they build around themselves. Shells are really one-room houses that molluscs build out of their own bodies. It's as easy for them to do this as it is for you to grow fingernails. Each shell has room for just one animal.

Molluscs eat tiny bits of food that float with the moving water. They also eat the **algae** that cover rocks. Part of this food is used to build their bodies. The rest helps them build their shells. A mollusc and its shell keep growing as long as the mollusc lives.

When a mollusc dies, it leaves behind its shell. That is why most of the shells you find on the beach are empty. Mollusc shells can last for thousands of years - a reminder of how long molluscs have been living on the Earth.

LEARN MORE! READ THESE ARTICLES...
CORAL • OCTOPUSES • SPONGES

Mussels, pictured here in a tide pool, are a kind of mollusc. Mussels are found all over the world, mostly in cool seas.
© Kennan Ward/Corbis

Answer: Snails, oysters, and squid are all molluscs.

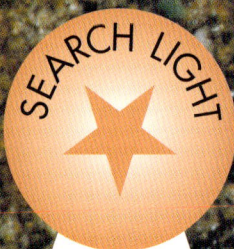

SEARCH LIGHT

What are two ways that an octopus can escape from an enemy?

Eight-Armed Wonders

People used to tell scary stories about a deep-sea monster that wrapped its many long arms around a ship and dragged it down to the bottom of the ocean. They called the monster a 'devilfish'.

Today we know that this wasn't a monster at all. It was an octopus - an animal with eight arms that lives in the ocean. Octopuses are members of an animal group called molluscs, which includes squid, clams, and oysters.

There are nearly 50 kinds of octopus. Some are only a few centimetres long. The largest is longer than 9 metres and may weigh more than 68 kilos. But no octopus grows large enough to attack a ship!

An octopus usually lives alone amongst the rocks on the bottom of the ocean. Sometimes it moves rocks with its long arms, or **tentacles**, to make a little cave for itself. On the underside of each of its tentacles are many little round suckers, or **suction** cups. These help the octopus climb over rocks and hold on to things.

Suckers on the underside of the tentacle of a giant Pacific octopus.
© Stuart Westmorland/Corbis

Octopuses like to eat shellfish such as crabs, lobsters, and mussels. An octopus will crawl about on its rubbery tentacles as it looks for food. But it can also swim very fast. An octopus sometimes hunts fish, chasing them until they are too tired to swim anymore. Then the octopus tightly wraps its arms around the fish and eats them.

But the octopus has enemies too. It usually tries to hide from them. Many octopuses can hide by changing colour to match the area around them. If that doesn't work, the octopus shoots black ink into the water around it. The cloudy water confuses the enemy and helps the octopus get away.

LEARN MORE! READ THESE ARTICLES…
DEEP-SEA LIFE • JELLYFISH • MOLLUSCS

An octopus has eight arms, or tentacles. Its name comes from a Greek word that means 'eight-footed'.
© Stephen Frink/Corbis

DID YOU KNOW?
Octopuses are very smart. In fact, next to dolphins and whales, the common octopus is perhaps the smartest animal living in the ocean!

Answer: It can change colour and squirt ink into the water.

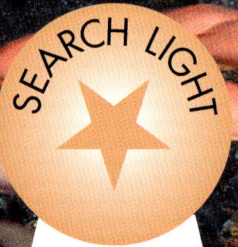

SEARCH LIGHT

Which of
the following
statements are
true about sponges?
a) Sponges can
be found mainly in
the sea.
b) Sponges eat by
straining the water
around them.
c) The sponges in your
house probably came
from the sea.

Plants or Animals?

Sponges are strange animals. They don't have the body parts - inside or outside - that we expect an animal to have. They don't even move around. Instead, they stay attached to an underwater rock or coral reef, just like plants. For a long time, people thought sponges were plants. Scientists decided that sponges are animals only after watching them eating food by drawing it into their bodies.

There are nearly 5,000 different kinds of sponges. Most live in the sea, but a few like freshwater. Sponges may be flat like spreading moss. Or they may look like trees with branching arms. Some are as tiny as a bean, while others are as tall as a person. Some are smooth and mushy, while others are rough, hard, and prickly. Some are dull and drab, while others are brightly coloured.

A sponge gets oxygen to breathe and food particles to eat by straining water through its body. Sometimes fish, shrimp, and other creatures live inside a sponge. A few sponges attach themselves to crab shells and go wherever the crab goes.

People dive to collect sponges or pull them up with hooks. Afterward the sponges are dried, cleaned, and trimmed. The fleshy parts are thrown away, and only the 'spongy' skeleton is used. The ancient Greeks and Romans used sponges to pad their armour and helmets. People still use sponges for scrubbing themselves clean, for painting, and for making medicines. However, factory-made sponges have taken the place of natural sponges in most homes.

© Stephen Frink/Corbis

© Royalty-Free/Corbis

(Top) Vase sponge; (bottom) marine sponges.

LEARN MORE! READ THESE ARTICLES…
CORAL • JELLYFISH • MOLLUSCS

A school of fish swims near some sponges. A few animals eat sponges, but most leave them alone because of their unpleasant taste and smell.
© Royalty-Free/Corbis

Answer: a) Sponges can be found mainly in the sea.
b) Sponges eat by straining the water around them.

SEARCH LIGHT

The African or Cape buffalo are large animals with large horns. They were once hunted to the point of being endangered. Why do you think people were hunting them?

In China, as in other parts of the world, water buffalo like this one help plough the field.
© Vince Streano/Corbis

Water-Loving Beasts

The American animal that most people call a buffalo is actually a bison. True buffalo live in warm places in Asia or Africa. The best known among them is the Indian buffalo. It's also called the water buffalo. That's because these animals love to lie in the water or in mud. This helps them to stay cool and keep the flies away. Buffalo eat mostly grass.

DID YOU KNOW? Mozzarella cheese used to be made from water buffalo milk. True mozzarella still is.

Asian water buffalo have been reared and used by people for many years. They carry loads and pull carts. Some help farmers to plough fields, especially in India and East Asia. But that's not all. Some people in Asia eat buffalo meat. They use its skin for making leather goods. Buttons, bangles and many other things are made from the buffalo's horns. And buffalo milk is rich and full of cream.

The water buffalo of Asia are heavily built and look like oxen. Some may be taller than 1.5 metres at the shoulder. The smallest buffalo are the *anoa* from Indonesia and the *tamarau* from the Philippines. They are just about 1 metre high.

Mud-caked buffalo in Kenya.
© Yann Arthus-Bertrand/Corbis

All buffalo have horns, but not all buffalo horns are the same. Some curve backwards. Some curve inwards. The Asian water buffalo and the African Cape buffalo have the biggest horns. The horns of the *anoa* are short and nearly straight.

Sadly, there are very few Cape buffalo left. They were thought to be dangerous to humans and have been over-hunted.

LEARN MORE! READ THESE ARTICLES…
HIPPOPOTAMUSES • WALRUSES • WHALES

Answer: Cape buffalo were over-hunted for two main reasons. First, hunters enjoyed having the Cape buffalo - like other large animals - as a trophy, mainly for its large horns. Second, people were afraid of the Cape buffalo and thought it was dangerous. So, like wolves and snakes in other countries, the buffalo were often killed on sight.

Kings of the River

Underneath the water in the rivers of Africa, a giant animal moves along the muddy bottom and eats water plants. It's named after a horse, looks something like a pig, and is larger than a crocodile. It's the king of the river, the hippopotamus. Its name is a combination of two Greek words that join together to mean 'river horse'.

An African folktale describes how God created the hippopotamus and told it to cut grass for the other animals. When the hippo discovered how hot Africa was, it asked God if it could stay in the water during the day and cut grass at night when it was cool. God agreed. However, he was worried that the hippo might eat the river's fish. The hippo, however, ate only plants. At night, hippos still go ashore and wander in herds, eating grass.

(Top) A herd of hippos in Botswana; (bottom) fully submerged hippopotamus.

Hippos have barrel-shaped bodies, short legs, and four toes on each foot. Adult hippos can weigh more than 2,700 kilos. The biggest hippos may reach 4.6 metres in length and stand 1.5 metres tall at the shoulder. Although the hippo looks clumsy on land, it is well equipped for life in the water. It swims easily, and when it stays underwater, little flaps of skin close its **nostrils**.

When a hippo is mostly **submerged**, the only things you can see are its rounded eyes, tiny ears, and raised nostrils. Sometimes a hippo lifts its head out of the water and roars. When that happens, you can see its enormous red mouth and very long teeth.

Because of the hippo's great size, its only enemies are lions and people.

LEARN MORE! READ THESE ARTICLES…
ALLIGATORS AND CROCODILES • BUFFALO • WALRUSES

SEARCH LIGHT

Find and correct the mistake in the following sentence: When a hippo goes underwater, it constantly blows water out of its nostrils.

A hippopotamus stands along the shore of Lake Manyara in Tanzania.
© Wolfgang Kaehler/Corbis

DID YOU KNOW?
Baby hippos are born in the water and can swim before they can walk.

Answer: When a hippo goes underwater, little flaps of skin close its nostrils.

The slow-moving manatee lives in warm shallow coastal waters. Because manatees can't see very well, they are often injured by motorboats in their feeding areas.
© Douglas Faulkner/Corbis

Mermaids of Yore?

Stories about mermaids tell of creatures that have the head and body of a human and the tail of a fish. These stories may have come from people who saw manatees swimming and didn't know what they were.

A manatee is a large stoutly built animal with a **tapered** body that ends in a flat rounded tail. Adults grow to about 3 metres long and 360-545 kilos. The manatee has a thick tough skin and is nearly hairless. It uses its flippers for turning, holding food, moving along the bottom of rivers, and holding its young.

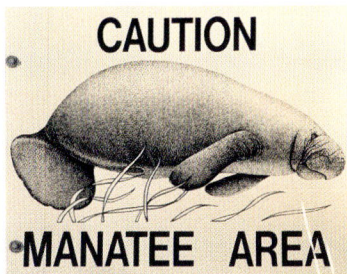

Manatees, especially the mothers and their calves, talk to each other using chirps, grunts, and squeaks. The other members of a group communicate by touching **muzzle** to muzzle. Manatees may live alone or in groups of 15 to 20.

Boater's warning sign.
© Catherine Karnow/Corbis

SEARCH LIGHT

Mother manatees and their calves communicate through
a) chirps, grunts, and squeaks.
b) snaps, crackles, and pops.
c) dings, rattles, and creaks.

They live in shallow waters along the coasts of oceans or in rivers that are rich in the plants they eat. The Caribbean manatee lives from the coasts of the southeastern United States to those of northern South America. The Amazonian manatee, as you might guess, lives in the Amazon River and other nearby freshwater. And the African manatee is found in the coastal waters and slow-moving rivers of tropical West Africa.

Manatees have small eyes and can't see very well. They don't move very fast either. Since manatees can't **tolerate** cool temperatures, they live in warm waters - places where lots of people like to live as well. Many manatees have been killed or injured when people drive their motorboats into the manatees' feeding areas. The manatees can't see the boats and don't move fast enough to get out of their way.

LEARN MORE! READ THESE ARTICLES...
HIPPOPOTAMUSES • WALRUSES • WHALES

Muskrats look like a cross between a rat and a beaver.
They live in water where they build a home of mud and
plants that rises above the water's surface.
© Scott Nielsen/Bruce Coleman

The Town Builders

Muskrats are ratlike rodents that look a little like small beavers and live in water. The animal gets its name from the two musk **glands** under its tail. The glands give off a heavy, musky smell. Muskrats were originally found only in North America. People took them to Europe and Asia about 100 years ago, and they soon made themselves at home in those regions as well.

Muskrats build their houses in water, as a part of a 'town'. Mounds of mud, bulrushes, and other plants are heaped up into a dome-shaped structure. This rises above the surface of the water. The animals dig tunnels from under the water up into the mound. They then hollow out a room at the top, a few inches above the waterline.

Muskrats also dig narrow **channels** through the surrounding plant growth. The channels connect to each other and to other mounds. Muskrats can sometimes be seen swimming along these channels. They feed on different kinds of **sedges**, reeds, and roots of water plants, as well as **mussels**, crayfish, salamanders, and fish.

Muskrats have small eyes and ears and a long scaly flat tail. They use the tail as a **rudder** for steering or changing direction while swimming. The hind feet are partially webbed and are used as paddles.

Muskrat fur is waterproof and keeps the animals warm. Muskrats continue to be trapped because of the quality of that fur. Because of that, there are far fewer muskrats today than there were in the past.

LEARN MORE! READ THESE ARTICLES…
MANATEES • MOLLUSCS • WALRUSES

SEARCH LIGHT

Are muskrats herbivores (plant eaters) or carnivores (meat eaters)?

Answer: Actually, muskrats eat both plants and meat, which makes them omnivores (animals that eat all foods).

SEARCH LIGHT

Fill in the gap: All walruses have _____ growing from the sides of their mouths that help them fight, cut holes in the ice, and drag themselves out of the water.

DID YOU KNOW?

The scientific name for the walrus, *Odobenus rosmarus*, translates into English as 'tooth-walking sea horse'.

The Whale Horses

In the cold Arctic seas of Europe, Asia, and North America, there lives a large creature called the 'walrus'. Its name is an English version of the **Scandinavian** word *hvalros*, meaning 'whale horse'.

The walrus has a stocky body topped by a rounded head. It has small eyes like those of a pig and a short broad mouth. Its mouth is covered with stiff whiskers. Every year, the walrus grows a new set of whiskers. An adult walrus can grow to twice the length of a Ping-Pong table.

Group of walruses gathered on rocks.
© Wolfgang Kaehler/Corbis

All walruses have long **tusks** growing on each side of the mouth. The tusks are very handy. The walrus uses them to fight, cut holes in ice, and pull itself out of water. Walruses spend nearly their whole life at sea. However, they often climb onto ice or rocky islands to rest and to have babies.

The walrus has flippers. In the water the flippers help the animal swim. On land the walrus uses them to walk. The walrus also uses its flippers to hold prey such as fish, but clams are its favourite food. Sometimes the animal feeds on young seals, though this happens only when it fails to find other food.

Walruses are social animals and live in groups of more than 100 members. There are two types of walrus, named for the two major oceans where they live: the Pacific walrus and the Atlantic walrus. The Pacific walrus is heavier and has longer tusks than the Atlantic walrus.

In the late 20th century, efforts were made to protect walruses. This helped increase the population of the Pacific walrus.

LEARN MORE! READ THESE ARTICLES…
MANATEES • PENGUINS • WHALES

Walruses are known for their long tusks. They use their flippers to help them walk on land.
© W. Perry Conway/Corbis

Answer: All walruses have tusks growing from the sides of their mouths that help them fight, cut holes in the ice, and drag themselves out of the water.

The Biggest Animals of All

Whales live in the water. They look like fish. They swim like fish. But they aren't fish at all. Whales are 'aquatic mammals'. 'Aquatic' means they live in water. Mammals are warm-blooded creatures that give birth to live young ones and feed them with milk.

Whales can't stay under the water all the time as fish do. They have to come up for air from time to time. They breathe through blowholes at the top of their heads. When their warm breath hits the colder air outside, it makes a cloud of mist called the whale's 'spout'. You can spot a whale by its spout.

Fish can't make sounds. But whales can make two kinds of sounds. The first sounds like a bark, or a whistle, or sometimes a scream. Whales make these sounds to speak to each other. Some whales also make very loud, low sounds that other whales can hear from many miles away. This sound can be heard only under water.

The biggest whale of all is the blue whale. It can be 34 metres long and weigh around 152 tonnes. That's more than ten buses put together! Even a baby blue whale is huge.

(Top) Killer whale; (bottom) beluga whales.